WHAT TO BE

WHAT TO BE

by
Steve Berman
and
Vivian Weiss

Prentice-Hall, Inc., Englewood Cliffs, New Jersey

Printed in the United States of America

Prentice-Hall International, Inc., London
Prentice-Hall of Australia, Pty. Ltd., North Sydney
Prentice-Hall of Canada, Ltd., Toronto
Prentice-Hall of India Private Ltd., New Delhi
Prentice-Hall of Japan, Inc., Tokyo
Prentice-Hall of Southeast Asia Pte. Ltd., Singapore
Whitehall Books Limited, Wellington, New Zealand

10 9 8 7 6 5 4 3 2 1

Library of Congress Cataloging in Publication Data
Berman, Steve
    What to be.

    SUMMARY: Explores a variety of careers through
interviews with a scrimshander, comic book dealer,
vocational counselor, chiropractor, massage therapist,
calligrapher, acupuncturist, potter, and others.
    1. Vocational guidance—Juvenile literature.
[1. Occupations] I. Weiss, Vivian, joint author.
II. Beim, Judy.   III. Title.
HF5381.2.B46   331.3′4   80-19149
ISBN 0-13-955278-2

This book is dedicated to Benjamin Pope, our ten-year-old friend and collaborator.

TABLE OF CONTENTS

INTRODUCTION

I'm thirty years old and a writer. But when I was your age, I thought there were only three things I could become when I grew up: a doctor, a lawyer, or a teacher. I thought that way because my parents thought that way.

I found out, though, that there were a lot of other things I could become. In fact, I found out that there were so many other interesting jobs—jobs I'd never even heard of—that choosing just one of them was very difficult for me.

Benjamin and I wrote this book to show you that there are dozens of interesting occupations; some, I bet, you've never even heard of. Did you ever meet someone, for example, who was a *calligrapher*? Or a *scrimshander*? Or a *dance therapist*? Or someone who made their living by buying and selling old comic books? Or a violin maker? Or even someone who sold home-made ice cream?

These are just a few of the people you'll be meeting in this book. There are dozens of others: a jazz singer, a chef, a television producer, a photographer, a potter, a furniture maker, a children's book writer. You'll get to know why and how each of these people became what they became. And you'll also learn a little about what these people do—how a professional photographer gets the pictures he's after . . . how it feels to be the singer in a fifteen-piece jazz band . . . or how a comic book dealer can sell just one comic book and make thousands of dollars.

If you already know what you want to be, then I hope this book will make you want to be it even more. But if you don't yet know what you want to be—and I bet most of you don't—then I hope this book will give you a lot of new ideas.

Steve Berman
Northampton, Mass.

1

INSTRUMENT MAKER

INSTRUMENT MAKER

Marten Cornelissen

All my life, since I was maybe five years old, I've been interested in trying to understand how things work. Things like why do birds fly or why do fish swim so well. I always had this scientific interest. As a kid, I remember spending most of my time building and designing model airplanes and sailboats. And they didn't have the sort of preassembled plastic kits they have today. For materials I'd go to sawmills and find old wood strips lying around.

Almost any boy has made model airplanes but I was really into it. I'd do research into what really made one of them tick. I always wanted to improve on it.

So for me, when I first held a violin—I was sixteen at the time—I found the structure of the violin highly interesting. Not just from a musical point of view, either. But why does a violin work the way it works. It's a box with some strings and yet somehow it produces sound. This was the same kind of thing as my fascination with model airplanes; to understand how it works.

I loved classical music. But my interest in making instruments was based on my scientific curiosity.

I started getting literature about this new interest of mine. There's a fine book published in Germany about violin making. I read the book and by following the instructions, I made my first violin. I used wood out of my family's barn. I was the type of person who really went at whatever he was interested in. It only took me a couple of weeks, I remember, to make that first violin. After that, I started visiting other violin makers to find out everything I didn't know.

People suggested that I go to violin-making school which is in Germany. But that was out of the question because it cost so much money and I didn't have any. So I just started making violins and showing them to musicians. Looking back on it, I think it was good that I didn't go to any of these special schools. I wasn't flooded with other people's ideas about how a violin should be made. I was able to develop my own ways. Also, I'm the sort of person who doesn't accept authority very well. I need to do things on my own.

When I first started making violins, everyone thought I was wasting my time. You see, I let all my other studies go. At the time, I was studying mechanical engineering in school. But I was just so intrigued with making violins. There was no stopping me.

Most violin makers I've met became violin makers because that's what their fathers were. But my own father never pushed me. He wanted me to do whatever I wanted to do. He let me develop my talents without any outside pressure.

Today, it usually takes me about 150 hours to make an instrument. So if I want to work forty hours a week, I can make a violin in four weeks. I myself work twelve to fourteen hours a day, seven days a week. Because so many people want my instruments, they have to wait four years for me to make them one. That's how busy I am. I usually charge $8,000 for a cello and about half that for a violin.

I'll tell you something; I wouldn't be surprised that even when I get to be eighty and I've made a lot of violins, there will still be many questions that haven't been answered for me about violin making. And that's what keeps it all so fascinating.

2

SCRIMSHANDER

SCRIMSHANDER

Andrew Bell

I've been drawing most of my life, ever since I was a kid. And scrimshaw is really just drawing on ivory, on the tusks of elephants. I only started being a *scrimshander*—that's what someone who does scrimshaw is called—a couple of years ago. I made a belt buckle for a friend by etching a design on a zinc plate and then mounting it on rosewood. Then I saw some scrimshaw in a craft's store and, because it was like etching, I decided to try it.

I didn't know where I could get hold of any ivory, though. I remember looking up 'Ivory' in the telephone book and there it was—a store that sold ivory. I called them and they said they had all kinds of ivory. So I went there and that's what started it all.

I've learned it all on my own. I did visit some of the whaling museums in New Bedford, Massachusetts, and in Newport, Rhode Island. These whaling museums have lots of scrimshaw on display because it was the oldtime whalers who first practiced the art of scrimshaw. Instead of elephant tusks, though, they used to carve on the teeth of whales. With very primitive tools, using just a sewing needle sometimes, they'd spend their spare time aboard these huge whaling vessels making scrimshaw.

As far as I know, there are about three thousand scrimshanders in the United States. Most of them carve pretty traditional things—either animals or ships out on the sea. I prefer carving human figures into the ivory. So my work is a little different from these oldtime scrimshanders.

I work sometimes three and a half months on one piece. It's very slow, exacting work. And that's one of the things that first attracted me to scrimshaw. I like working slowly, meticulously.

People are amazed at the detail you can get on the ivory. But after a day's work, my hands and my eyes are both tired. You'd be surprised at how hard you have to press into the ivory in order to scratch it.

The elephants use their tusks for pushing and digging. So by the time I get them they have to be polished. Some of these tusks can be as large as eight feet long and a foot in diameter at the base. They sell for about $8,000. Someone once told me, and it amazes me, that about a million and a half pounds of ivory come into this country every year from Africa. Fortunately, they don't have to kill elephants just to get the ivory. They wait for the elephants to die natural deaths and then collect the ivory.

3

ICE CREAM
PARLOR OWNERS

ICE CREAM PARLOR OWNERS

Gary Schaefer & Barbara Fingold

GARY: We were both social workers before becoming ice cream parlor owners. We'd been social workers for a number of years and both of us were a little bit bored with that. We felt like we wanted to have more options in our lives. So about a year ago, we started talking about changing our professions.

BARBARA: It was an amazing coincidence. Just at the time we'd decided to do something different with our lives, we found out that our favorite ice cream parlor was being sold. We got back from a vacation where we'd been discussing changing our careers, and the first thing we heard—from a friend who'd been watering our plants—was that this wonderful store was being sold. Well, we both looked at each other and instantly knew what our next profession was going to be.

GARY: We were both passionate ice cream lovers. One of my bad habits was having a bowl of ice cream every night before going to sleep. But to tell you the truth, I've almost grown not to like ice cream anymore. Maybe because I'm around it so much, I've lost my craving for it.

BARBARA: We always appreciated good ice cream. We always bought the best commercial ice creams. But now, since our store only uses homemade ice cream, even those really good brands you can buy at the supermarket just can't compare with our product.

GARY: But besides the fact that we both loved ice cream, there were other reasons why we went into this business. Ice cream, from a businessman's viewpoint, is a safe product. Good ice cream has been something people have always appreciated and bought. It's not like a clothing store, for example, where the fashions are always changing. Every six months there's a new style the public wants. Ice cream is not a fickle product. Also, the store we bought had already been a successful business. Everyone in our community loved the place. It was almost like a town meeting hall. Lawyers would have meetings there, the mayor would sometimes stop by. Our ice cream parlor was, and still is, a local institution.

BARBARA: Our parlor is not a big, faceless place. If somebody doesn't like something, they just come right over to us and tell us. And we've made a lot of friends through the store. People just come in, talk for awhile, eat a little ice cream and then resume their day's schedule.

GARY: It hasn't been easy, though. We had a lot of struggles when we first bought the place: Problems with employees, problems with machines breaking down, money problems. And most of all, the long hours. For awhile, we didn't have any time off. But I'm happy the way things turned out. It would be hard for either of us to now go back to some job where we had to work for somebody else. Even though we spend a lot more time with our own business than we'd spend if we worked for someone else, it just doesn't feel the same. We're choosing to do it now, instead of having to do it.

BARBARA: Mostly, owning an ice cream parlor is fun. And I really think that the customers who come into our store are the nicest people in town. There's something about the sort of people who seek out homemade ice cream. These are people who really have an appreciation for the better things in life.

4

CHILDREN'S BOOK WRITER

CHILDREN'S BOOK WRITER

Jane Yolen

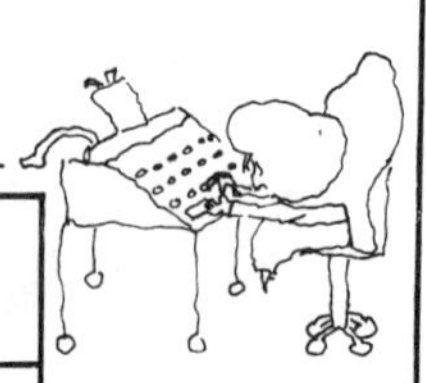

I think I always knew I wanted to be a writer. I always liked to write stories. My father's a writer and my mother was too and just about all the people my father was friendly with were writers.

The writers I met as a child were all exciting people. I'd read their stories, I'd hear them on the radio, and we had their books in our house. All of that reinforced in me the desire to become a writer.

My mother and father always praised me whenever I wrote anything. Plus, I was a great reader. I was one of those readers who read everything. But fairy tales were my favorite. I loved fairy tales. I adored them. I loved princesses with long braided hair.

Writing came easily to me at first but I realized as I grew older that to do it well I couldn't do it the easy way. Someone once said to me that if I wanted to be good at writing, I'd have to work hard even when I didn't want to.

Everyone always asks me how do I get the ideas for my stories. I don't have a teacher telling me what to write about like you, somebody saying write about your summer vacation. I don't have anyone telling me what I should write about. So I have the entire universe to pick from.

Another writer, a friend of mine, when he was asked that same question said, "I get my ideas in the mail." Now that's a joke but the point is I <u>can</u> get my ideas in the mail. Someone might send me a letter and it can give me an idea. Or I can get an idea by listening to a rock group.

I don't really know where my next idea is going to come from but I can tell you where some of my past stories have come from. I wrote one book called RAINBOW RIDER and that story came from a song I heard by the rock group THREE DOG NIGHT. They have a song called "Joy To The World" and one of the verses mentions a rainbow rider. Now a lot of people heard that song. But after hearing the song, how many people then wrote a book called RAINBOW RIDER. That song started something in me. And if you're a writer, then once you hear something or see something that says something to you, then you ask yourself the question—<u>what if</u>. What if there really was a rainbow rider. That's how a story begins.

Writing is really like a sport. The more you do it, the stronger your writing muscles get and the better writer you become. If I stop writing for awhile, it's not good because my muscles get slack. So I'm better at it now than I was when I was younger.

People find it hard to believe that I really enjoy writing. That's because writing is something we're all made to do in school and most of us don't enjoy it. Maybe some people can understand how I can enjoy writing a story once. But the idea that I rewrite and rewrite and rewrite the same story, well, most people don't even like to change a spelling mistake.

I try to work on my stories until they're just right. I'm not saying that I always find the rewriting—the going over the same story five, ten, or even twenty times—a total joy. But I do love writing.

5

COMIC BOOK DEALER

COMIC BOOK DEALER

Norman Witty

I collected comic books when I was a kid and I started collecting them again in the middle sixties when I was about twenty-five years old. I was riding on a bus across the country and that's when I started reading *Marvel Comics*. I loved them. They were totally different from the comics I'd read as a kid. They seemed much more sophisticated, especially *Spiderman*.

Anyway, when I finally got off the bus in Los Angeles, I started going around to all the old bookstores looking for the comics I'd loved as a kid. There were a lot of shops in California doing business in comic books. And the old comics I'd loved as a kid, I saw, were getting pretty expensive. They were becoming collector's items. That's when I started buying comic books as investments.

I had a friend who was running a comic book shop in Los Angeles and I learned the business from him.

In the late forties and early fifties, when I was a kid, I used to buy *Donald Duck, Dick Tracy,* and *Mad* comics, and I always collected all the old issues I didn't have. I wanted these older comics because the old comics had the best quality. The quality of the early *Dick Tracy* comics, for instance, was much better than any of the newer ones. And one of Disney's artists did the really funny, really beautiful duck comics. I loved his early *Donald Duck* comics.

Today, I have a huge collection of duck comics, and a lot of the *Dick Tracy* and *Mad* comics. So the same comics I used to own as a kid, I now have again. But it's taken me a small fortune and years of collecting to get them back.

I went through the same experience a lot of kids go through. I had a huge collection. But when I went away to college, my mother threw all my comics out. I'll tell you, my mother and I had a rough time when I found out she'd thrown out my comics.

I make a good living buying and selling comics. Most people find that amazing. They don't believe that comic books are thought of as antiques and that people are willing to pay large sums of money for them.

In the early sixties, I was once at an auction. A house was being sold and everything in the house was being auctioned off, including some comics from the early forties. There were about forty of them and they were in perfect condition. They'd been stored in the attic. Well, I paid fifty dollars for these forty or so comics. These were very early *Batman* and *Superman* comics. They were some of the best drawn comics ever. Well, I ended up selling most of these comic books for around $2,500. In fact, I still have a handful of them left, and these are probably worth at least $1,500.

I always thought that this business would be a comfortable, enjoyable business for me, considering how much I love comics. Only one thing upsets me: I've discovered too many dishonest comic dealers who take advantage of kids. They'll sell them junky comic books, making out like they're expensive ones. I've seen guys give kids five cents for their old comics, then turn around and sell the same comic to some other kid for two, three, even four dollars. It's ok to charge twenty-five cents for a comic you bought for a nickel. But charging three dollars is another story. I guess I feel a real allegiance to kids. I don't want them to be ripped off, but you'd be surprised how many people over-charge kids for comics.

6

DOCUMENTARY FILMMAKER

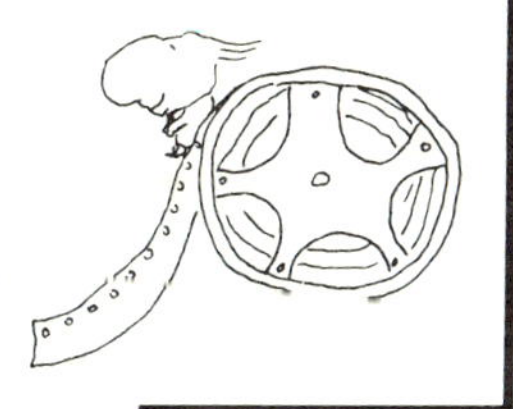

DOCUMENTARY FILMMAKER

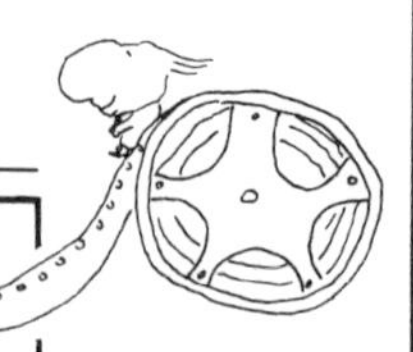

Abbie Waze

I didn't even know what a documentary film was when I was growing up. So it wasn't as if I'd always dreamed of becoming a documentary filmmaker.

A documentary film is a movie that's about real people, about real situations. There are no actors or actresses in them.

A lot of different things led me to becoming a documentary filmmaker. First, I met a man a few years ago who'd been making documentary films and he was very inspiring. He was making a documentary film about his grandfather when we met. I think the whole idea that I could use my own experiences and then share them through a film was very exciting to me.

In college, I studied anthropology. I would study different cultures, different types of people. And learning about people who were very different from me was wonderful. When I then realized I could learn about different types of people by making movies about them, I started to learn everything I could about how to make a movie.

I try to show in my movies what people's lives are all about. And the people I make movies about are usually people who our society doesn't really care about. I've made movies about mental hospital patients. I also made a movie about a refugee family from Viet Nam who are now living in America. And right now, I'm in the middle of shooting a film about girls from poorer sections of New York City. I want to show that these are all people we can learn from if we just take them seriously. Most people don't think these people have any dignity. But in my movies, I try to show that's not at all true.

Making movies makes me feel good about myself. And through my movies, I hope people will be able to understand me a little bit better.

What really drew me to this work—and what makes it all worthwhile—is that it allows me to become very involved in the lives of the people I'm filming. My relationship with the people I'm filming is the most important thing for me. It also determines if any of my films are successful or not. The more involved I am in the lives of these people, the more honest are my films.

7

VOCATIONAL COUNSELOR

VOCATIONAL COUNSELOR

Amy Kahn

I'm a vocational counselor. That means I try to help people figure out what kind of job they want and what kinds of jobs they can do well.

The majority of the men and women in the United States will have to work the majority of their lives. When you think about that, then work becomes very important. It's how we spend most of our lives. Or at least how we spend a good portion of our lives. So if we don't like the work we do, then we're not going to feel happy. And that's what my work is all about: helping people to stop and think about their careers rather than just rushing into some work that's without meaning.

In your life, you'll ask yourself this question many times: What type of work do I want to do? Most people, according to national averages, change their careers four times in the course of their lives. Consequently, nobody has to feel that they have only one shot at choosing their life's work.

Did you know that there are over 20,000 different types of jobs in this country? There's a book called *The Dictionary of Occupational Titles,* which is put out by the Department of Labor in Washington, D.C., and it lists all those 20,000 different types of jobs. Most people can probably only name a hundred types of jobs. They don't have a sense of all the variety.

When I first graduated from college, I had a hard time finding a job. I found myself well-educated, with lots of ideas and lots of ambition. But I just didn't know what to do. I struggled and I tried to figure out what kind of career I wanted. I asked myself, 'Do I want to be a teacher?' I was qualified to be a teacher. But I didn't really want to do that.

I went through that kind of job search many times in the years that followed, trying to figure out just what I wanted. Eventually, I decided to go back to school to become trained as a guidance counselor. I thought I'd like to work in a high school as a guidance counselor. But after my training, I couldn't find a job in guidance counseling. So then someone told me about a job opening in vocational counseling. And it really hit me as being perfect for me. I had been unemployed and looking for work probably five times by that point. So I knew what it felt like to be out in the job market, to be looking for something I could really put all my energies into. I felt I could really help people do that. I'd learned through my own experiences.

I now work with people who really don't know what they want. They may have had other jobs in the past that weren't satisfying, or they may have outgrown their work. I also work with people who've never had any previous jobs—people who don't even know what types of jobs they can do.

I find it an exciting process, helping someone to find meaningful work. In the process, the people I work with end up learning a lot about themselves and a lot about the world.

If I were speaking to a young person, someone who was ten or eleven years old, the first thing I'd want to tell them is not to worry about what they're going to become. They have a long time before they have to make a decision. Also, the more you get to know yourself, and the more you get to know what you like to do, the better you'll be able to make that decision when the time comes. So if you have interests, read about them, create hobbies, and talk to people about them. But don't worry about your career. When the time comes, you'll be prepared.

8

NEWSPAPER PUBLISHER

NEWSPAPER PUBLISHER

Geoffrey Robinson

I became a newspaper publisher totally by accident. I didn't plan on it at all.

During college, I thought I was going to become a doctor. So I took pre-med courses. Then I started applying to medical schools in my senior year. But I started collecting rejection letters.

So there I was—stuck—at the end of college. Everyone else knew what they were going to do. Some of my classmates were going to law school. Others were ready to go to work for some large company. But me—I was totally stuck. I really had no idea what I was going to do.

A friend of mine was moving to Ohio and I decided to go out there too. I had to decide on some job, some job that would be reasonably interesting. Well, one of the first things I thought of was a newspaper job because I was always intrigued by newspapers. I'd always liked reading newspapers.

Fortunately, I happened to get a job on a newspaper out in Ohio. That was my first job.

After that job, I got another job with a much bigger newspaper. I was an editor which meant I read the stories the reporters wrote and then fixed them up a bit.

I worked for a large daily newspaper. It was a morning newspaper and that meant that all the work had to be done at night which was one reason I couldn't stand it. Newspaper jobs are really strange. You go nuts. For a morning paper, all the work is done between five in the afternoon and two in the morning. So I'd get to work right when everyone else was leaving for home. It made me feel like I was totally backwards. I was constantly out-of-whack with the rest of society.

I worked these weird night hours—editing stories, writing headlines, deciding what stories should be made big, what stories should be made small, picking pictures to go with the stories—and some nights I actually put the type on the page.

But I found myself getting tired of the job. It was very repetitive. And that's when I decided to start a paper of my own. I started it with a couple of friends and because we started it, we wound up being in charge of it.

We had an idea: to put out a small weekly newspaper in an area that didn't have one. Now we didn't really know how to do it. We'd never done it before and no one had taught us. And I'd never even planned on doing this sort of thing. But we thought we could think it out. So it became a challenge to actually make this concept work. Thinking of something that isn't there and then creating it was, for me, the most exciting part.

It's like an inventor. You get an idea, then you draw it on a piece of paper, and then you're just dying to put it all together and see if it actually flies. That's what I loved about it.

When we started the paper, it was a lot of fun and we spent all our time getting the paper out. We'd work seven days a week, sometimes around the clock. It was the most challenging and exciting thing I'd ever done.

All of us who started the paper sweated it out together. And it was the first time I had fun like that since I was really little.

I work less hours now. I don't keep up the kind of breakneck, six-and-seven-day weeks I did before. I'd drop dead if I did. But there's always something new, so I'm constantly busy.

I never planned on doing this. It sort of just happened. As for the future, again I have no real ideas about what's going to happen to me. I just don't have any long-term plans. I sort of fly more by the seat of my pants and take it as it comes.

9

CHIROPRACTOR

CHIROPRACTOR

Leonard Cohen

In the late nineteenth century, there lived a man whose name was D. D. Palmer. He wasn't a medical doctor, but he was very interested in healing people who were sick. In the apartment house where Mr. Palmer lived, there was a janitor who was hard of hearing. One day, D. D. Palmer asked this janitor how he'd become hard of hearing. "About fifteen years ago," the janitor said, "I bent down to pick something up and I heard a pop in my back. After that, my hearing went." D. D. Palmer, being a very inquisitive person, then asked the janitor if he could look at his back.

So D. D. Palmer looked at the janitor's back and no one knows exactly what happened but apparently he found an area that looked as if it was out of place on the janitor's spine. "Gee," D. D. Palmer muttered. "That's probably the area where you heard the pop."

Somehow, by using only his hands, D. D. Palmer then massaged the man's spine, and within no time at all the janitor's hearing had returned. And that's the way *chiropractic* started.

Now manipulating the spine with only your hands—and that's really what a chiropractor does—is a very ancient art. I've seen two thousand year old carvings showing people manipulating someone's spine. So obviously, this form of healing has been around a very long time.

I have to explain a little about how the body works for you

to understand how chiropractic works. Inside your head, there's your brain. And attached to your brain is a column of nerves called your spinal cord that goes all the way down your back. Now in order for nerves to get from your spinal cord and your brain to all the other parts of your body that they control, these nerves have to first leave the spine. And they leave your spine through *vertebrae,* small openings in the bony part of the spine. There are a couple dozen vertebrae.

Well, if those vertebrae are misaligned, if there's something wrong with them, then that can cause the nerve messages that your brain is sending out to not flow smoothly. And if those messages from your brain can't get through your spine, problems are going to arise. Stated more simply: If there's a problem in the flow of the nerves through your spine, then your body can't respond to things the way it should.

My job as a chiropractor, simply stated, is to make sure these openings in your spine are working correctly. And my only tools are my hands.

You have to go to a special school to become a chiropractor. It's very similar to medical school. We study everything they study in medical school except surgery and drugs. Since we don't use drugs or practice surgery as chiropractors, there's no need for us to study those areas. And like medical school, we have to go to school for four years.

People don't know a lot about chiropractic. There are no television shows about chiropractors, the way there are about doctors. Most of the people who become chiropractors usually have some firsthand experience with it. They may have had some back problems when they were younger and were helped by a chiropractor. Or someone in their family was once healed by a chiropractor. That's how most of the people in my class became interested in chiropractic.

10

ILLUSTRATOR

ILLUSTRATOR

Tom Leamon

As long as I can remember, I've always drawn pictures. My mother still has the first picture I ever drew. It was a picture of a spider. I was three years old, I think, when I drew it.

When I was in the second and third grade, I was sick a lot. I had a lot of ear trouble. Almost every winter I had an operation on my ears. So my father would come up to my room where I was sick and draw with me. You know, I'd be in bed for a long time and he would come up at the end of the day and draw with me. That's really how I got started.

All through school, I was the *Boy Wonder*. Everybody would come over to me and say, 'Look what Tommy drew.' It was sort of my road to fame while I was in school. Everybody knew me as 'The Artist'.

Back then, I liked to draw people. I'd draw my grandfather or my father. I'd ask them to sit down and I'd sketch them. And the pictures really looked like them.

Then, when I was in the eighth grade, one of my teachers became very interested in me. Every Friday night she took me to a course in cartooning at a nearby college. So there were a lot of people who encouraged me all along the way.

After high school, I went into the army and worked for an army newspaper doing illustrations. Then I went to an art school, the Rhode Island School of Design, for four years.

I call myself an illustrator which really means I do a number of different things. I'm a political cartoonist—meaning I do a lot of caricatures of political figures. A caricature is usually a funny picture of someone, a picture that exaggerates someone's features or gestures. I also do illustrations for children's books and I've done illustrations for adult educational books. I've even designed labels for a label company. And once, I made masks for a children's theater group. So there's quite a range of things I like to do.

I love the independence of being a freelance artist. Freelancers don't work for any one person or company on a full-time basis. And that arrangement suits me best. I've always liked to work by myself. I don't like other people telling me what to do. I work best when I can carry out my own schedule.

Probably the hardest aspect to what I do is getting consistent work. Sometimes it comes in great bunches. I'll have a couple of books to illustrate, some newspaper assignments, some magazine assignments and my time will be absolutely crazy. But then there'll be a period of a month or so when I won't have any income. And that's very difficult. You have to get used to not always having a steady income.

And sometimes it's hard to work alone. I'll get to looking at one of my pictures and sometimes I just can't tell anymore if it's good or bad. I need some other artists to tell me what they think about it. I've been able to solve that problem by meeting every month with a group of artists. We try to offer our honest feelings about each other's work.

11

CARPENTER, FARMER, MECHANIC, GREENHOUSE FOREMAN

CARPENTER, FARMER, MECHANIC, GREENHOUSE FOREMAN

Roger Smith

When I was about thirteen years old, I was like a lot of other kids my age. I thought I knew exactly what I wanted to do. I always thought I wanted to be a carpenter. My father was a carpenter; so I thought I wanted to be one too.

But when I got a little older, I started working on a dairy farm. I was actually running a dairy farm for someone else and going to school at the same time. This was during high school. I would get up in the morning at about five o'clock, do all the chores—milk the cows, clean the barn, make sure everything was all set for the milkman to pick up the milk, feed the chickens, get the cows out to pasture—and then I'd go to school. And after school, I'd change my clothes and hop on my bike and go up to the farm and do the same things all over again. So I started to think that maybe I'd like to be a farmer.

But after thinking that I might want to be a carpenter, and then a farmer, I began discovering that I wanted to be a mechanic. Everyone I knew—and this was towards the end of high school—wanted a car. So I decided I was going to take the mechanical course at the nearby vocational school.

I spent four years there and I was all set to work as a mechanic after I graduated. I even had a job lined up. But again, unexpected events changed the course of my life. One afternoon, a neighbor whose father had recently died needed some extra help at his farm. So I went over there to help him do his chores. Well, it turned out that this man liked me and I liked him. And he eventually asked me to work for him full time. And what he offered me in dollars and cents was far more than what I could earn as a mechanic. So I had a big decision to make. Would I stay with the trade I'd just spent four years learning or would I switch and go back to farming?

After a lot of soul-searching, I decided to become a farmer again because I loved that type of work. And my carpentry and mechanical skills wouldn't be wasted. A farmer needs to know how to do a little of everything.

I worked at this farm for over nine years. I was the foreman. It was a large dairy farm. We had over a hundred milking cows. But running a farm—paying the taxes, the insurance—was starting to be too costly. And I started to see that there wasn't too much of a future for me in farming. But I loved the work.

Well, just about that time, another of those unexpected events came into my life. A man approached me and asked me if I'd like to run some greenhouses at a nearby college. He knew I was a farmer which meant to him that I was a good worker. Well, this was really one of the biggest decisions I ever had to make. Would I leave the farm which I loved so much or would I take up a new trade and work at the greenhouses?

I'd already changed my occupation a few times—from a carpenter to a farmer to a mechanic and then back to a farmer. Would I again change my profession? It was a big decision but I decided to try the new profession.

But how could I run the greenhouses at a college after being a farmer? I'd never studied anything about growing plants in a greenhouse. I knew nothing at all about how greenhouses worked. But I just decided I'd learn everything I could learn.

I really believe that a person can do anything he or she wants to do if they want to put themselves into it. You hear people say, 'Well, if you want to be president, you can be president.' Well, that doesn't mean you can be the President of the United States. But if you really put your heart and soul into something—if you want to study, if you want to work—then you can do just about anything you want.

I remember a teacher I once had who told us we'd all have three, maybe even more jobs in our lives. He said each of us would change our professions at least three times. I didn't believe him at the time. I used to think that a person could only be one thing in a lifetime—that whatever job you were doing when you were twenty, that's what you'd be doing at fifty. I now know differently. And I also know that choosing a career isn't always a logical process.

12

MASSAGE THERAPIST

MASSAGE THERAPIST

Patricia Wachter

Six years ago, I was given a massage by a friend. She was massaging my face. I'd never had a massage before. I didn't have any idea what it was about. While I was getting this facial massage, I could feel my jaw start to relax. It just felt like it dropped to the floor. I looked at my friend and said, "What was that?" And she said, "You just relaxed." I was so amazed by this experience of relaxing my body that my curiosity was awakened. And I wanted to see if I could do that to someone else, to make them feel that relaxed.

So I started massaging all my friends' faces. And I discovered that I liked to touch people and I felt I had a good touch. I felt really good when I massaged people.

I didn't read any books about it. I just kept exploring with my hands. It was a process of self-learning, of self-teaching.

At first, I didn't know that people made their livings by giving massages. But when I found out that I could, I was very interested because doing this sort of work felt so natural to me.

I then went to a school and took a course in Swedish massage. This is a method of massage that was developed in Sweden a couple of hundred years ago. I learned how to feel a little more in control of what I was doing at the school. I learned a technique there.

Massage goes all the way back to the early Greeks. Because of their athletic ability and interests, the Greeks developed a system of how to take care of their bodies—and massage was part of that system.

Massage is more popular today in Europe than it is in America. For Europeans, a massage isn't a luxury. It's a necessity. A lot of Europeans get massaged once a week. It helps them to stay healthy, to feel relaxed, and to stay alert.

When I first started doing massage, it was like being an athlete. I ached. My hands ached. My neck ached. I had to get my muscles developed to a certain level.

I, too, get massaged once a week by another massage therapist. When you give massages all week—and I sometimes give as many as twenty a week—it's important to get a massage for yourself.

13

DISC
JOCKEY

DISC JOCKEY

Charlie Pellett

I became a disc jockey purely by chance. It started off in high school. I was a senior and there used to be a group of students who read the announcements over the school's public address system in the mornings. I thought these kids who read the day's announcements were pretty awful and I thought I would do a far, far superior job. So I went up to the office and found out that it was pretty much a random process for choosing who read the announcements. If you showed up at eight in the morning, then you had the job. You know, you'd talk into the public address system, announcing that the girl's volleyball would be meeting or that the boy's basketball team would be selling candy after school to raise money.

So one day, I did it. And I was shocked to find all the kids in the homeroom happy to have had a representative from their room announcing the day's events. And then, many, many kids in the school suddenly knew who I was, people who didn't know. I was a transfer student then, and so the immediate recognition was nice.

That's how I first started talking into a microphone and reaching a large number of people.

Then I went to college and I wanted to get involved in an extracurricular activity. And because I had this high school experience, I sauntered on down to the student radio station. People down there and I found a highly receptive group of people who were willing to take the time to answer my stupid

I was one of the few people willing to show up at two in the morning—after the station had signed off the air—to learn about all the equipment. And there was so much to learn.

I started off answering phones for my college radio station. If people needed rides somewhere or if their animals were missing, they'd call in and I'd take down their message. Eventually, from just answering phones, I got involved in the news department at the radio station. And by the end of my freshman year, people there thought I was doing a good enough job to appoint me the station's news director.

I then asked a local radio station near where I went to college, if I could do an internship with them. I simply offered them my services in order to gain some experience and some additional knowledge about radio broadcasting. I did the summer internship and had a fun time doing that. I even filled in for the afternoon news person on occasion.

I finished up my degree at the university and I then took a job at the local radio station where I had once interned. And today, I'm on the air from seven to midnight, playing lots of music, and broadcasting the news, weather, and sports.

I listen to a lot of radio. I haven't watched television in ages. I wake up in the morning and I listen to everything from 'beautiful music' stations to 'Top Forty Rock n' Roll' stations, to classical music stations. I try to find out what everyone else is doing. And I listen to myself on tape. I think that's where I learn about how to control my voice. But unlike some disc jockeys, I never had any formal broadcasting education. Everything I learned, I learned by myself.

The roughest thing for a person getting involved in broadcasting is getting that first job. That's the hardest part, the major stumbling block. But there are thousands of radio stations across the country and many, many stations hire people right off the streets. Very little experience is needed.

There's a fair amount of technical knowledge that's required. But it really isn't that much. You know, you go into a radio station and you see masses of equipment all over the place. But I could probably show you how everything works in a half hour.

If people are thinking about a career in radio, there are a couple of ways I would recommend to get into it—and I would recommend them in this order. First, I'd recommend going to a four year college with a fairly good radio station. If family circumstances or economics don't permit that, you can go to a broadcasting school. You'll find that tuition is fairly high but it will definitely pay itself back. Also, in the armed services, you can get stationed at a base that has its own radio station. Even on some large Navy ships, they have their own closed-circuit radio and television stations where you can learn everything you need to know.

I just want to add that women should think about careers as disc jockeys. More and more stations are now looking for women disc jockeys. It's not just a man's field.

14

KARATE
INSTRUCTOR

KARATE INSTRUCTOR

Chester Holubecki

When I first got out of college, I worked as a bookkeeper. But I didn't want to work behind a desk all day. It just didn't feel right.

I'd gotten involved with judo at a local YMCA. I studied there for about nine months, and then a friend of mine introduced me to a karate school that wasn't too far from where I lived. So I took up the karate courses and eventually, after a lot of hard work, I received the black belt, the highest level of achievement in karate.

Karate is basically learning how to defend yourself. It's a defensive art consisting of blocking and punching. It was developed in China by the Buddhist monks. They learned all these fighting techniques by watching animals fight.

It took me eighteen months to earn my black belt. When I first took it up, I used to go out to the *dojo*, that's the arena where karate is done, and I'd work out five or six times a week. The average person, though, works out an average of only two or three times a week. So it takes the average person anywhere from three to four years to make a black belt.

It's not easy to become a black belt, though. In all my years of teaching—and I've been teaching for nearly ten years—I've probably had about 1,200 students. And up to this point, I've only had about a dozen black belts.

In karate, there are different stages until you reach the highest stage, the black belt. It's just like going through elementary school, junior high school, high school, and then college.

White belt is the beginner's belt. Then, the major belts you strive for are green, brown, and finally, the black belt.

I think every kid should know karate—and the younger the better. It serves many purposes. It teaches someone how to defend himself. It's also great for physical fitness. And it keeps your weight down, improves your coordination, and also helps build up self-confidence.

I didn't start studying karate until I was twenty-one. I was already an adult when I started it. I thought I had a career as a bookkeeper. But I found out that being a bookkeeper wasn't for me. I didn't like sitting at a desk all day.

15

MOVIE THEATER OWNERS

MOVIE THEATER OWNERS

Richard Pini & John Morrison

RICHARD: I got fired from a job. I was a college French teacher. It took the fact of me not having a job to start me thinking about doing something I'd never thought of doing before. I'd been a teacher all my life and had never thought of doing anything else. Owning a movie theater never even crossed my mind.

I'd always enjoyed movies, though. All my life, I'd gone to the movies at least once a week. And when I was a French teacher, I used to teach a course about French movies.

I met John, my partner, through an organization that showed movies at the school where I taught. And we talked about how much fun it would be to own our own theater. When I found myself out of a job, our talks became more serious. That's when we actually started looking for a theater.

JOHN: I became the owner of this movie house almost for the same reasons that Richard did. I also lost a job and I was also a teacher. But I didn't enjoy teaching. The three years I was a teacher were probably the most miserable years of my life.

I ran a film series at the school where I taught and that's what started me thinking about one day owning my own theater. I was showing two or three different movies a week and I loved it. But when I was fired, I realized I wouldn't be able to see all these movies anymore. And by that time, I was addicted to movies. I knew I had to do something; owning my own theater seemed like the thing to do.

I, too, always loved movies. When I was young, I used to watch television. I lived in a rural town and the nearest movie house was probably twenty miles away. So I watched a lot of movies on television. I loved watching these movies and my mother would often come in and see me watching a movie on some station where you could hardly see the film because there was so much interference. She'd tell me I was going to go blind if I kept watching these stations that had such bad reception.
RICHARD: The hardest thing about owning your own movie house is standing in the lobby when no one's coming in to see the film. You think you have bad breath and that you're scaring people away. What's most fun is showing the films you like and seeing the audience liking them too.

We choose all the films we show. Fighting with John about what these films are going to be is really the most fun.
JOHN: That's the most important aspect of our business—deciding on what movies we're going to show. You can have the best advertising in the world, the bathrooms can be kept perfectly clean, but if the movies you're showing are bad movies, then you're not going to have anyone coming into your movie house.

16

JAZZ
SINGER

JAZZ SINGER

Bev Rohlehr

Everybody in my family was into singing. We'd always sing together as a family. Whenever we'd go on trips, we'd all sing in the car. I remember I was always accused of singing flat. But that never seemed to bother me. I loved singing too much to let a little criticism get in my way.

Seriously, though, I always knew I was a good singer. And I have good ears, meaning I can hear something once and then I can sing it right away.

I sang in the choir in elementary school and in church, and then in high school and in college. But I never actually said to myself—until much later—that I was going to be a singer. I didn't know what I wanted to be. I even dropped out of college because there I was, spending a lot of money with no idea what I wanted to do.

It was pretty hard for me to become a singer because everyone in my family was either a doctor or a lawyer. My grandmother is even a lawyer which is pretty amazing considering she's a black woman. It wasn't easy for a black woman back then to become anything, especially something as difficult as a lawyer.

Today, whenever I see her, she tells me music is no career for a woman. Only my mother has stood by me. She's always supported my wanting to be a singer.

After I left college, I played in a lot of rock 'n roll bands. But I still hadn't really made up my mind that music was going to be my life. Then, in the fall of 1972, I finally made the decision. I remember the day I said I was going to be a singer. It was a cold day in November. I was putting asphalt shingles on a roof to earn some extra money. My fingers were freezing. It was drizzling. I remember saying to myself, 'Self, what are you doing here? There's gotta be another way for you to earn a living.' Then, I said to myself, 'Self, you can sing.' And that was it, that was the day. Right after that I formed a band and I haven't stopped singing since.

Jazz is the music I love most. It's the most challenging. And I find that jazz musicians are almost always much better musicians than rock 'n rollers. When I sing with jazz musicians behind me, I can feel them pushing me to put out my best. It's never boring.

The only hard thing about being a jazz singer is that sometimes you get nervous in front of an audience. It's hard when you sing with a big jazz band because if you make a mistake, it really stands out. . . . But I've found out that you survive. I made a mistake the other night, a bad one. But I saw that I could still live to talk about it the next day.

If you really needed to know why I became a jazz singer in one word, then that word would be *fun*. I do what I do because it's fun.

17

CALLIGRAPHER

CALLIGRAPHER

Jim Sadler

The word calligraphy means 'beautiful writing.' And that's what a calligrapher does. The way I wrote my name at the top of this page is an example of calligraphy.

Calligraphy can be either beautiful handwriting or very formal lettering. And the thing that makes calligraphy so beautiful is the constant contrast between thick and thin lines. You need a special pen to get that contrast, a broad-tipped pen. You can't get that sort of effect with just a regular ball-point pen.

Look at the lettering at the top of this page. Take the *A*, for example, in my last name. You can see that some of the lines forming that *A* are thin, while others are thick. But with a regular pen you couldn't get that sort of variation in the thickness of the lines.

I didn't become interested in calligraphy until I was already in art school. I was studying to be either a painter or a graphic designer. Calligraphy was one of the courses you had to take in order to meet the school's requirements. Well, I took the class and I absolutely hated it. I hated it so much that I wanted to leave the class. I already knew how to draw but I just couldn't do calligraphy at all. No matter how hard I tried, everything I did was just terrible. But I had a very good teacher who encouraged me to hang in there—which I did. And then I started loving calligraphy.

I teach calligraphy and I do it commercially. Often, people will want me to design a wedding invitation for them. I've also written wedding documents, the actual marriage contract between two people. And I do a lot of posters for different events, things like concerts and plays.

Before there were printing presses everything was written out by hand—books, legal documents. But in the fifteenth century, when printing was invented, calligraphy died because it was no longer really useful. Printing was easier and cheaper. As a result, there were very few people practicing calligraphy for hundreds of years.

But today, more and more people are becoming interested in calligraphy. They're appreciating how beautiful it can be. If you've ever gotten a letter from a friend who wrote the letter in calligraphy, then you know how special it can be.

What's interesting to me is that I always had terrible penmanship when I was in elementary school. Even now, when I write quickly, it's very difficult for people to read my handwriting. And I've heard that's true for a lot of calligraphers.

A lot of people think that calligraphy, no matter who's doing it, will always look the same. But that's not true at all. It always depends on who's doing it. Everyone has their own style. And you can tell a lot about someone by the way their calligraphy looks. Who you are really comes through in your work.

18

MACROBIOTIC CHEF

MACROBIOTIC CHEF

Paul Sustick

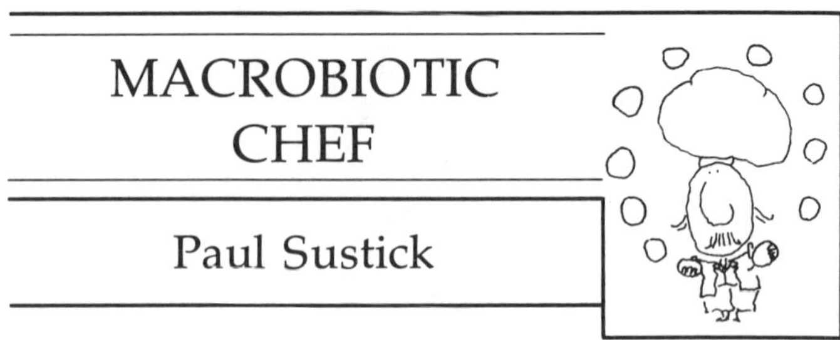

I never thought when I was young that I'd own a restaurant or be a chef. But there was a time in my life when I was in desperate need of a job and the opportunity to become a chef presented itself.

I cook macrobiotically. That's a big word but basically all it means is that I try to cook very simply, using foods that aren't filled with unhealthy chemicals. Most of the meals I prepare consist of vegetables, a grain (like rice, millet, or buckwheat), and sometimes fish.

I worked four years, training to become a chef. And that's not really a long time. The man I learned from had to study for ten years. He was a Japanese man and he studied in Japan.

The Japanese style of teaching starts you out by doing the lowest job. So the first few months of my training, all I did was get down on the floor and scrub all the dirt off the floors. Cleaning and washing dishes was really all I did. Then, I was allowed to do some of the other jobs, like making salads and doing some short-order cooking. So by the time my training was over, I'd done just about every job you can think of in a restaurant's kitchen.

It was just like going to school, except my school was a restaurant. During the day, I learned by watching my teacher working in the kitchen. Then, at night, we'd have classes. My cooking teacher would give us lectures. This training method is very old. It was used in Japan for centuries. You'd probably call it an apprenticeship today—that's when you study with a person for a certain amount of time and learn directly from them.

The nicest thing about owning a restaurant and being a chef is the feedback you get from the people who eat your creations. When people compliment the food, that's a wonderful feeling. That's what makes it all worthwhile. What's hard about running a restaurant, though, is that you work very hard. I get to the restaurant at seven-thirty in the morning and I don't leave until eleven at night. So I don't have too much free time.

We bake our own breads and pies. We cut all our vegetables by hand. And none of our food is frozen or made somewhere else. In order to serve natural, healthy foods to our customers, we have to put in a lot of time cooking and baking.

19

BOOKBINDER

BOOKBINDER

David Bourbeau

Bookbinding is an art that wasn't practiced for a long time. When machines were invented that could bind books, book-binders went out of business. But recently, in the past ten years, people who bind books by hand are becoming popular again. All the book arts, in fact—and that includes people who design, illustrate, print, and bind books—are coming back.

Books were always important to me. I lived in the country when I was growing up and the winters were long and we weren't near any towns. Books were all we had and every night we'd spend an hour or two, after dinner, reading. So I always loved books. But I never thought about the printer who printed the book, or the binder who bound the book.

I actually came to all this through painting. All my early schooling was aimed at my becoming a painter. When I got a little older, I fell in love with the work of a particular artist and decided I wanted to study with him. I met with him and that's when I discovered this new world, the world of printing, illustrating, and binding beautiful books. This artist was involved in this sort of work. He owned his own printing press.

I fell in love with the whole idea of creating beautiful books. And since I always loved books, I started to collect these fine press books. Eventually, I got the idea that I'd like to learn how to bind books. But I wasn't thinking then of becoming a professional bookbinder. I only wanted this to be a hobby, not a profession.

All this time, I owned a leather shop. I made sandals,

shoulder bags, and belts. But I was getting a little bored with my leather shop and I wanted to do something different. So a few years ago, I decided to study bookbinding full time. I sold my business and started studying with an old German bookbinder. I was his apprentice. I'd work all day with this man, learning how to be a bookbinder; and at night, to support myself, I'd work as a waiter. I did this for two years, until I felt I could start my own bindery.

The book you're now reading was bound by a machine. It probably took the machine just a few seconds to put this book together. It takes me anywhere from thirty to forty hours to bind a book, and that's before I even start to decorate its cover. But a book that's been bound by hand is going to be more beautiful than a book that's been bound by a machine.

A lot of the books I bind are old books that need to be restored. Some of these books are over four hundred years old. Because of age, they're falling apart and it's my job to put them back together again. I also bind special books that are written and illustrated by contemporary artists. These are called 'limited edition' books and that's because only a couple of dozen of them are printed at a time.

To bind a small book, I might charge around $175.00. I usually work with leather. I also use gold to decorate the leather covers of my books.

Right now, I'm restoring a sixteenth century book about philosophy. It comes from the rare book room of a nearby college.

20

TELEVISION PRODUCER

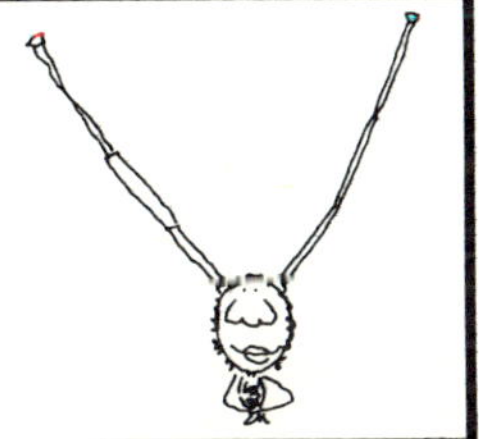

TELEVISION PRODUCER

Carol Cashwan

When I was very young, I had this fantasy that I'd someday be a movie director. But when I was a little older it was journalism that interested me. So after I graduated college, I became a newspaper reporter.

But that was hard work for me because I couldn't sit down with myself for a long time. I wasn't real comfortable being alone so much, and that's what a writer's life is all about. I found out that I needed to work with people. Plus, newspapers didn't pay very well.

My newspaper work, though, did prove to be a good background for a career in television.

If you're interested in working in television, you really have to be willing to do just about anything when you first start out. My first job in television was as a secretary. Then, I became a researcher for a news show. I'd investigate a news story—a teachers' strike or a tenant-landlord battle—and then I'd tell the on-the-scene reporter all the information I'd gathered. I'd actually stand under him as the cameras would be rolling, feeding him the information he needed.

After awhile, I thought I might like to be the actual reporter, the person you see every night on television. But everyone I spoke to thought I was too young looking.

People say you need a break in order to get into television. Mine came when I was asked if I'd like to be on the staff of a new show that was just starting to air. I was asked to help produce the show, a half-hour news program.

I have a lot of power now working behind-the-scenes of the show—more than if I was a reporter. Basically, I tell the reporters what stories to cover. So I've learned that it's the producers who determine the contents of the show, not the reporters.

The good thing about working in television is that it's so broad. It's not like an industry. It's more like a world. It's like putting yourself and your talents into a whole community of people. And whatever you're interested in—entertainment, news, sports—it's all there.

The bad thing about television, though—and this is something I always forget—is that it's a business. Every show has to appeal to as large an audience as it can. Otherwise there won't be any advertisers to sponsor the show. And unfortunately, this makes it hard sometimes to produce interesting shows. Too often when you try to please everybody, you end up pleasing no one.

21

ACUPUNCTURIST

ACUPUNCTURIST

Jonathan Klate

I'm sure *acupuncturist* is a new word for most of the people reading this book. An acupuncturist practices acupuncture. And acupuncture is one of the oldest forms of healing known to mankind. It originated in China nearly five thousand years ago.

So I practice a very ancient form of medicine. In fact, the main book I've had to study from was written in 400 B.C. It's called *The Yellow Emperor's Classic of Internal Medicine.*

I think the fact that this form of medicine is still being practiced speaks well for the laws and principles upon which it's based.

This form of medicine doesn't only concern itself with a person's body. It's interested in the mind and the spirit of a person, as well.

But how did someone who was brought up in the United States end up studying an ancient form of Chinese medicine?

Well, my mother was very sick. She'd been suffering with an illness for a long time. And none of the doctors she'd consulted could cure her. One of my sister's close friends was an acupuncturist and he treated my mother. And he cured her. My mother was really rejuvenated in a manner I thought truly remarkable. Her whole personality seemed to be affected by the treatment.

My father, who's a doctor, then decided to learn more about this ancient type of medicine. He went to England and studied at The College of Chinese Acupuncture. So it was through my father that I became more and more interested in acupuncture.

Acupuncture treatment is usually carried out by inserting very fine needles into specific points of the body. The needles vary in length from one to four inches and they're usually inserted just below the surface of the skin. The lower legs, the feet, the forearms, and the hands are where the needles are usually placed. During a treatment session, I'll use anywhere from three to eight needles.

These needles, unlike the injections you receive from your doctor, don't hurt. There's very little pain really when the needles are inserted into the skin.

Knowing where to place these needles is one of the things you're taught during your training.

Now when some people even hear the word *needle,* they cringe. But these needles are nothing like any needles you've ever had. There's nothing in the needle or on the needle. There's nothing that's put into your body or taken out of your body with these needles. They're narrow, sterilized, stainless steel needles. You don't even bleed when they're inserted into your skin.

Medical doctors in America and Europe are just beginning to take this ancient form of Oriental medicine seriously. A handful of western doctors, like my father, have even started studying acupuncture.

It takes a considerable number of years to learn acupuncture and many, many more to become an expert. The Chinese consider that it takes up to ten years to become technically competent and much longer to become a master of acupuncture.

22

CLOTHING DESIGNER & DRESSMAKER

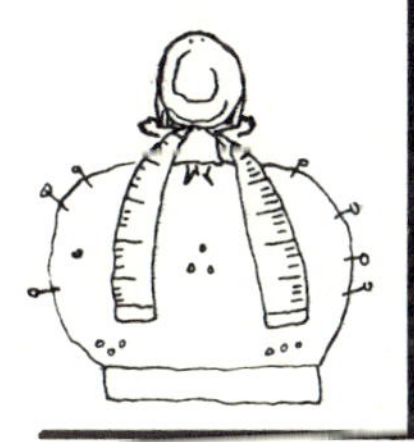

CLOTHING DESIGNER & DRESSMAKER

Judy Fine

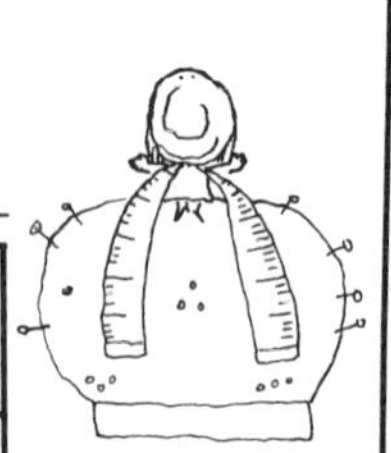

I got started in this field when I started making dolls' clothes. I was a little girl and because I loved my dolls, I wanted them to have nice clothes. My mother certainly wasn't going to buy me all the clothes I wanted for my dolls. So I made them myself. I'd take a piece of fabric, punch two holes in it, and stick my dolls' arms through it.

Designing and making clothes became my business when I lived in Texas. There were very few job opportunities where I lived in Texas and I had to find some way of making a living. I lived on a beach and you could drive your car right onto the sand. So I made bathing suits and set up a van and drove the van right onto the beach and peddled my clothes. And that started people saying, 'Well, I don't want this but do you make clothes?' And I started getting orders. I made waitress uniforms for a restaurant. I made skirts, blouses, dresses. I made mostly women's clothes then. I hadn't yet learned tailoring which is the art of making men's clothes.

I should mention that for thirty years my grandmother was a saleswoman in a clothing store and that my mother's always been very fashion conscious. So clothing and fashion were a part of my growing up. But because I had clothing and fashion hammered into my head as a kid, I actually hated it for awhile. I totally rebelled. From eighteen to twenty-three, I wore the ugliest, sackiest things I could possibly wear. I didn't realize I was rebelling at the time. But after that phase, I came around to loving it again. And now I really love it.

I now design and make custom clothing. That means people come to me because they want something made especially for them. If they go into a store, usually they won't get something that fits them perfectly. But if I make them a dress or a pair of pants, it'll fit just right.

Also, the clothes I make are of the highest quality. But unfortunately, the clothes you buy today in most stores are terribly made. They're actually made to fall apart—so that in about a year's time you'll have to go out and buy something new. They're made to last just one season.

You see, you should sew with twelve stitches to every inch of seam. But store-bought clothes only have six stitches to every inch. So if one stitch opens up, your whole seam opens up. And if you don't sew, you just stick it in the closet and then you have to go out and buy something new.

Time doesn't exist for me when I sew. I can start at eight o'clock in the morning and the next thing I know, it's five at night. And every day is different. There's no real routine. I'm always sewing but I'm always sewing a new piece of clothing.

There's only one real problem with what I do; my customers sometime expect too much of me. Because they're having clothes especially made for them, they expect a miracle. They want their clothes to make them look beautiful. If they're fat, they want their clothes to make them look thin. Of if they're too short, they want my clothes to make them look taller. They just don't understand that it's not the clothes they don't like. It's their bodies.

I never wanted to be a teacher, or a lawyer, or a nurse. I just always loved sewing.

23

DANCE THERAPIST

DANCE THERAPIST

Elaine Raskind Chitel

I studied ballet for many, many years when I was very young. But then I stopped, and I didn't take any more dance lessons until after I had my own children.

At about that time, I was also becoming interested in psychotherapy. Psychotherapy has to do with feelings and working things out that you have a lot of conflicts about. If you feel stuck about something, or if you feel you can't do all the things you'd like to do, psychotherapy can sometimes help you.

I eventually decided that I wanted to do some kind of work that would involve therapy and also my background in dance. So I put dance together with therapy and found out there was a profession called 'dance therapy.' At that point, I decided to go back to school and get a graduate degree in dance therapy.

Dance therapy is a pretty new profession. It started in the 1940's. Until the 1940's, really crazy people were locked up in hospitals and they were shackled down. They were actually physically contained so that they wouldn't hurt themselves or hurt other people. It was like they were prisoners in a jail. But a woman named Marian Chace, a dancer and a dance teacher who lived in Washington, D.C., had the idea that maybe these people could be helped by dancing, by moving their bodies. So she went to the back wards of these hospitals and worked with very old and very, very chronic people. Chronic means people who've been mentally ill for a long time.

These were people who didn't know who they were. They didn't know what they were all about. They couldn't really talk very much, either. But they were able to move. And so this woman who started dance therapy got these people to dance in groups and she saw how much these people were helped by her movement classes. That's basically how this profession began.

There are a lot of different types of people who can benefit from dance therapy. Old people living in nursing homes, chronic patients in mental hospitals, blind children, mentally retarded children, and physically handicapped children can all be helped by dance therapy.

Dance therapy is just beginning to get the kind of recognition it really deserves. But the salaries aren't very terrific and the work is exhausting.

24

PHOTOGRAPHER

PHOTOGRAPHER

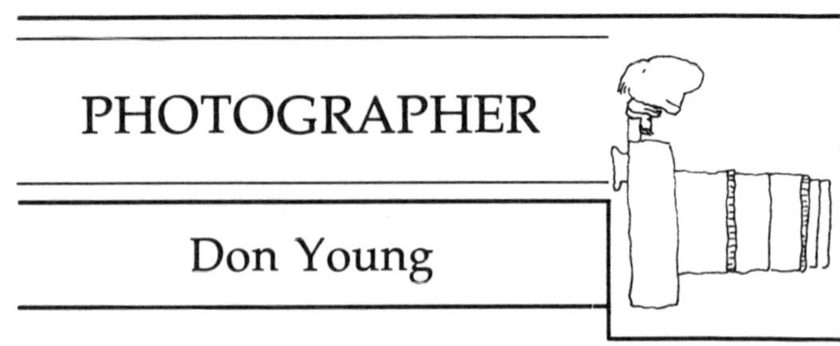

Don Young

At one point in my life, I had to make a decision about what I was going to do. And it just so happened that right about that time, I was using a camera and I happened to get something on film that was very marketable. It was a photograph of the entertainer, Sammy Davis Jr. I just happened to be at the right place at the right time. The newspaper I now work for ran that photo as its cover shot. That's when I first started thinking about making money with a camera.

I never had a photograph published until that day. There was absolutely no planned effort by me to become a photographer. It just happened.

I always liked photography. I just never thought of it as a profession. My interest in photography started when I was ten years old. My grandfather gave me a camera, a little Brownie. I used it all the time. Whenever my parents needed a photograph taken of the family, they'd ask me to do it. I was also my junior high school class photographer.

I'm what's called a photojournalist. I use my camera to document events.

A lot of people think that being a photographer is a very exciting job. Well, it is. You meet so many people and you're always involved in what's happening. But it's also a lot of very hard work.

The hardest thing about being a photographer is that you're constantly dealing with people. And some people just don't want you to take their photo. At a rock concert, for example, the musicians might not want you to take their pictures. They don't need the publicity and they have other things to do. But if my newspaper wants that picture, I somehow have to get it.

I usually try to photograph happy faces. I'll even make people laugh just to get them to smile. And there's one thing I won't do: I'll never photograph someone smoking a cigarette. I don't want to encourage people to smoke cigarettes.

25

POTTER

POTTER

Bob Woo

I have a lot of cousins and they're all doctors or lawyers. So it was expected of me to go into a profession. And because I was always a good student, I think my father just assumed I'd go into something that was more established.

My father was, naturally, very disturbed when I decided to go to graduate school in pottery. "Where's pottery going to lead you?" he asked me. He really wasn't able to understand what I was doing with my life. He respects me today, but I think he's still not sure why I chose to do what I do.

The rewards of being a potter are different from our society's more accepted rewards. For one thing, you usually don't make a lot of money being a potter.

When I first got to college, I majored in physics. But I realized I just didn't have the discipline for that. So I goofed off and got horrible grades. Then, I decided to major in philosophy. But at a certain point, I realized I wasn't going to be a philosopher nor was I interested in teaching philosophy—which are the only two things you can do with a philosophy major.

But I had been taking some art courses on the side and one of these was pottery. And I had a great time with all these art courses. So when it was time for me to decide what I wanted to do with my life, I applied to graduate school in art.

I wanted to make pots. That was my dream. And graduate school was the only place where I could get that much experience in making pots that quickly. It was faster than apprenticing. And it was faster than trying to pick it up on my own.

When I left graduate school, I had a choice again—either to teach pottery or to become what's called a production potter, which is someone who throws pots and then sells them for a living. Since my dream was to have my own pottery studio and to throw pots, I decided production pottery was best for me.

When you first learn how to do pottery, being able to get the clump of clay centered in your hands is hard. But then it becomes second-nature. It's like athletes. Athletes can do certain things by second-nature that other people have to think a long time about. Pottery's like that. The more you do it, the easier it is to do. And the more fun it becomes.

26

"MR. GRANOLA"

"MR. GRANOLA"

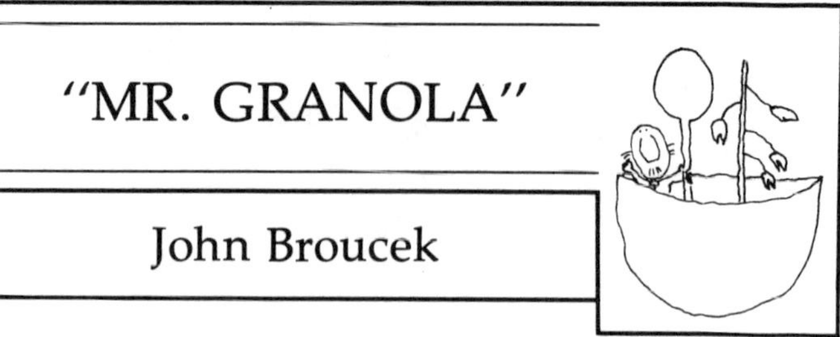

John Broucek

President of the
GOOD MORNING GRANOLA COMPANY

I used to be a house painter. I loved it because it was work I could do outside. But I was always splashing thinners, turpentines, and paint all over my body. And I knew my skin didn't like that. So I very much wanted to work with natural materials, with things that would be good for my body.

So when a friend one day asked me if I wanted to start a granola-making company, I liked the idea.

Granola is a healthy breakfast cereal that's made from oats, wheat bran, honey, oil, maple syrup, vanilla extract, dried fruits and nuts, and cinnamon.

Years before I went into the business of making granola, I used to eat it all the time. But the granola I'd buy in the stores never had enough fruits or nuts in it. I was always adding my own ingredients to these store-bought granolas. I'd put in sunflower seeds, raisins, and almonds. So the first thing I did when I started my own granola business was to make a granola with everything in it, a granola that was chock full of fruits and nuts. I was set on making a granola that didn't need anything added to it before you ate it.

Our business grew slowly but surely. We used to make about two hundred pounds of granola a month. Now we're making close to ten thousand pounds a month. And people all throughout New England, Pennsylvania, New Jersey, and New York buy our product. We're even thinking of making granola bars, granola cookies, and granola donuts.

I'll walk around town and everyone will call me "Mr. Granola." They just come over to me and say, 'Good morning, Mr. Granola.' And I guess I like that because I never tell them that's not my real name.

27

MIME

MIME

Jody Scolese

There's no way I ever could have guessed I would have been in theater, especially mime. I didn't know what a mime was for twenty-five years. I love my parents but they didn't know about theater or art. So they couldn't make that world available to me. Their ideal for me was to get a job as fast as I could—a job where I could make as much money as I could.

After I'd been in college for awhile and had spent four years in the Air Force, I decided to go back to school. I went back just for the fun of it. I wanted to take courses I'd never taken before. So I took an acting class and a dance class. I'd never done anything like that before. I'd never done anything on a stage before, never performed in front of people. But I knew I always had an urge to create. I just never knew what to do with that urge.

I then saw a mime company and I'd never seen a full-fledged mime company perform. Well, the next day I called the company up and said, 'I don't know how this sounds but I know I can be a mime. I want to be one. And I know you must get a million people who call you up with this same silly attitude. But I really want to try to be in your company. If there's an opening, I want to try for it.' And there was. They needed a few extra people for a new show they were developing. So I auditioned and I got it.

After that, I heard about a mime who was also a teacher, and I ended up taking his classes. This teacher knew what pantomime was all about and I really learned from him.

Pantomime means doing silent skits. You use some props, sometimes some music. But you never say anything. It's all done silently.

There are sad mimes and there are happy mimes. Basically, your attitude about life comes through in how you perform. Now I have an attitude about what life is all about and so that's what comes through in my work. It's about how people see themselves. People want to think they're cool, and they're slick and nifty. But no matter how hard you try to think you're important or wonderful, there's always something that makes you look totally ridiculous. You know, you might be all dressed up. You might have the feeling that you're really something special. But then there's this big booger on your nose. So that's kind of how I see the world and that's how my performances say something about people.

A mime's duty is to make people laugh at themselves. And whatever I portray on the stage—a happy or sad situation—I'm always trying to entertain my audiences.

Very few people know what it's like to be on a stage, to be performing in front of people for an hour and a half. It's sometimes very scary. You have to pay very close attention to what you're doing on the stage. People won't laugh or they won't cry if you're not really involved with what you're doing. It just won't work. So it takes a lot of concentration and a lot of training to be a performer.

Being a mime is sometimes scary. In some ways, it's a whole lot easier to go to work every day at some regular job. You have a certain amount of pay that somebody pays you for a certain amount of hours. The good thing is that you know you're going to get your money and you can pay the bills. But it's bad, at least for me, because I know I'd go nuts having someone telling me what to do all the time for forty hours a week.

When you're growing up, people ask you all the time, "What do you want to be?" That question will drive you bananas. So if anybody ever asks you that and if you don't yet know what you want to be, just tell them it doesn't matter. And just don't worry about it. That's the last thing you should do—worry about it. I didn't figure out what I wanted to do with my life until I was in my late twenties. So just don't worry about it.

28

SECRETARY

SECRETARY

Marianne Donohue

As a secretary, the person you work for is essential. If they're dedicated and hardworking, then you better be dedicated and hardworking, too. You can't help but be excited when you work for an exciting person. So that's something I want to tell anyone who's interested in becoming a secretary —work for someone who cares about what they're doing. It will make your job a lot more meaningful.

The job I have now is like no other job I've ever had. I wish everyone could be this happy with their work. I'm the mayor's secretary. I've been so busy the last few weeks that my refrigerator at home is empty. I haven't had time to even grocery shop.

Working in the city government is a real education. The phone is constantly busy. And when someone calls here, they expect immediate service. So I have to be able to direct people to the right person so they can get their answers. In a sense, people don't think of me as simply being a secretary. I'm part of the mayor's office and with that comes a lot of responsibility.

I've been very unhappy in some of the jobs I've had. I know what it's like to not want to get up in the morning and go to work. But here, I come in early and I stay late. And that's because I feel like I'm part of a team, a team that's doing worthwhile things for the people of this community.

When I graduated from high school, I decided I'd continue my education. I went to a two year college and completed my associate degree. I took a medical secretary course there and

I liked it. The specialized aspect of not just being a secretary but of having some expertise in the medical area was appealing to me.

I would strongly discourage anyone who's taken a commercial course in high school from just going out and getting a job. I really think that, at least, a two year college education is very beneficial. Many people will tell you that it's not necessary to go to college if what you want to be is a secretary. But it would be very hard for someone to specialize in an area—like being a medical or a legal secretary—without some advanced training. Sure, you could go to work in a doctor's office as a receptionist. But you couldn't be a medical secretary. You wouldn't know medical terminology. You'd be looking words up in the dictionary all day long.

In the medical or legal field—and I've worked in both—a secretary can do very well. They can make as much money as social workers and teachers.

I haven't met very many male secretaries. But there's certainly no reason why a man couldn't do this job. If you can type, take shorthand, and answer phones, then it doesn't matter what sex you are.

29

FURNITURE MAKER

FURNITURE MAKER

Kristina Madsen

When I was in my last semester of high school there was a program whereby if you had finished all your credit work, you could find something else to study for six weeks. So I tried to find a woodworker at that time but I didn't have any luck. I just thought that's what I'd be interested in doing. It was just an inkling. But I don't really have a good answer for 'Why did I become a woodworker.'

My father is not at all handy. But I did discover since I started woodworking that on my mother's side, going right back to our earliest ancestors, there's always been someone who was a woodworker. So it must be in my blood because so many of my ancestors were woodworkers. Also, my last name is Madsen and in Scandinavia there are a lot of Madsens who are furniture designers.

I began studying with a master furniture maker about four years ago when I was eighteen. He had a workshop in a potato storage barn. We struck up an agreement whereby I would study with him for a year. I was in my first year of college when I met him and so I left college and started my apprenticeship.

I studied with my teacher for four years and last summer he hired me to be a teacher at the school he recently started. I teach now two days a week and I work on my own projects four days a week.

During those four years, I learned both furniture making and design. I now design all the furniture I make. Sometimes

I'll sketch a piece of furniture, make a clay model of it, then draft it—which means to make a scale drawing of it—and then, finally I'll start working on the piece.

When I first started out, I followed other people's designs, and that provided training for me to develop my woodworking skills.

I can do most everything a man can do. Sometimes when there's lumber to be hauled, I don't lift as much weight as a man. But as far as handling tools, I can do whatever a man can do.

30

FIREMAN

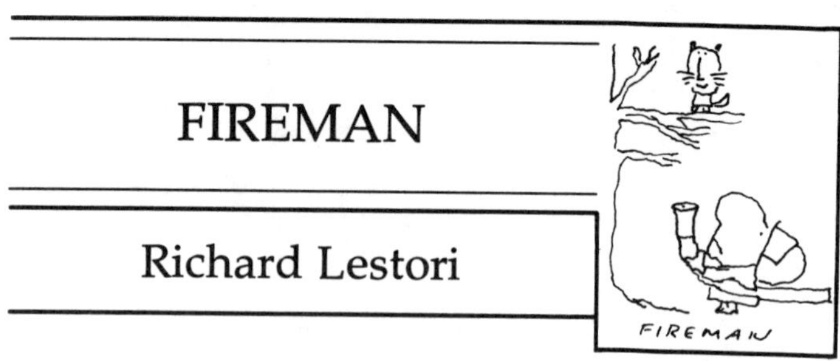

FIREMAN

Richard Lestori

I became a fireman because my father was a fireman. He used to take me to his firehouse when I was a kid and those were the most exciting times for me. I think I always knew I wanted to be a fireman.

There's an excitement about this job. When you're out there battling a three or four alarm fire, when you're right inside a building and the smoke is so thick that you can't see a foot in front of you, that's what it's all about.

It's a dangerous job. I've seen buddies of mine, guys I loved, killed in fires. And that's the roughest part of this job. The guys you work with are everything. It's like a football team. Everybody has to do his part.

It's the firemen, not the trucks or the water hoses, that put out a fire. You can have the best equipment in the world but without a group of skilled firemen, forget it.

I work in a very busy firehouse. Rarely does a day go by without our company making dozens of calls. A lot of the calls, though, don't pan out. They're false alarms or maybe just small fires that are extinguished by the time we get there. But then there are those times when the sky is red, when you can see the flames five blocks away. And when you work on one of those fires—well, in ten minutes you've already done more physical work than most people do in a month.

I can't tell you what it's like to be inside a building that's burning. There's fire all around you. There's thick smoke. The ceilings are caving in. And it's just you against that fire. Your buddies are in there trying to ventilate the building, trying to get the smoke to clear out. They're using hooks, axes, and halligans—breaking down doors, smashing out windows, anything to open up the building. And you're there, on the knob of the hose, getting that fire to die down.

Later, when we've put out the fire, the firehouse is like a locker room after a Super Bowl victory. The guys are up. Everyone's telling their own version of what happened back at the fire. And that's when you really feel part of a team. You always depend on the guy next to you in a fire. And you're depending on him for everything—for your life.

Believe me, sometimes it's slow. You sit in the firehouse and nothing's happening. You read, watch some television, talk to the guys. And on one level, you don't want a fire. You don't want to have to risk your life. You don't want to see your fellow fire fighters have to risk theirs. But on another level, you want that fire. You almost become addicted to that sort of life and death situation. That's when every part of you has to be alert. That's when you know you're doing something important.

31

VETERINARIAN'S TECHNICIAN

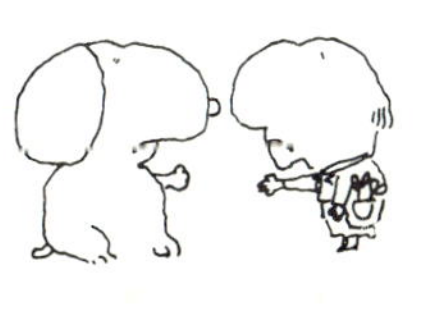

VETERINARIAN'S TECHNICIAN

Annette Szczygiel

When I was little, I wanted to be a veterinarian. I've always loved animals. But becoming a veterinarian requires a lot of education. And, for me, four years of college followed by four years of veterinarian school was just too much. So when I heard about a program at my local community college, a two year program that trained people to become veterinarian technicians, I applied for it and was accepted.

I didn't want a regular desk job. I wanted to do something that was a little different. And I wanted to work with animals.

Being a veterinarian's technician is like being a nurse for people. All the lab work is exactly the same as you would do for people. And we assist in surgery, as far as prepping for surgery—scrubbing the animals, getting all the materials ready, even monitoring the anesthesia. That's very interesting. You really have to be on your toes when you're making sure the anesthesia is going well. In addition, we help to restrain the animals when they need to be examined, and there are the receptionist's duties—answering phones, making appointments, keeping the office tidy.

It's the little puppies and kittens that have to be here for a couple of weeks that I really get attached to. When they pull through, it's a wonderful feeling. Seeing a scared, sick animal get well is my work's greatest satisfaction.

I try to give all the sick animals a lot of loving care. I always go over to them and pat them and talk to them. I think that sort of attention helps them to recover faster.

This can be a very physically strenuous type of job. You have to lift dogs onto a table in order to examine them. And some of the dogs weigh anywhere from eighty to a hundred pounds. And even if an animal isn't too heavy, it can become very wild. They don't want you to hold them.

The hardest part of this job is when people come to us and want us to put their animals to sleep. The doctors do this by an injection. It's painless. It's a high dosage of barbiturates. The animals literally fall asleep and then die. But it's sad to see that. I try not to be involved in that as much as possible. If it's a very sick animal, it's not that bad. But if it's a healthy animal, then it's really terrible. If someone finds a dog that's without tags and if the other animal shelters in the area can't find a home for it, then we have to put it to sleep.

Unfortunately, being a veterinarian's technician is not a very good paying job. Most people who go into the program know this. You have to really like what you're doing because the pay isn't too much. Sometimes it's only minimum wage.

You find out just how much you like working with animals. For some people, it's a stepping stone to becoming a veterinarian. For others, it's a permanent job.

32

BASEBALL SCOUT

BASEBALL SCOUT

Ralph Dennis

A baseball scout is a guy who's always on the lookout for new talent, for young players who might have a shot at the majors. So I spend a lot of my time watching young ballplayers—high school, college, and minor league players—to see how they throw, how they hit. I watch them at their positions. I see how a centerfielder gets under a ball, or if a pitcher has a solid fastball. If a guy has an ok fastball, then we can teach him the rest.

I'll tell you what I look for the most: hustle. When I was a player—and I played for eleven years in the minors—the ballplayers really went at it. But today, I just don't see that. Today's ballplayers aren't as hungry as they used to be. They're good ballplayers, some of them even great. But they just don't put out 110% each game.

So that's the sort of guy I'm after. The kid who eats, drinks, and sleeps baseball. Pete Rose—there's the ballplayer I want. Pete Rose isn't, at least in my eyes, the most perfect ballplayer around. A lot of guys can do what he can do. But the guy has guts. He takes what he has and he pushes it nonstop. Every time he's on that ball field, he's churning it out.

Between the ages of thirty and forty, that's when a baseball player starts to lose his greatness. He can still look trim, still have all his coordination. But those extra special reflexes, those reflexes that once allowed him to be in the majors now start to pass. So at thirty-five, most guys have to leave the game. A few of the players, though, like me, don't want to hang it up. We love the game too much to leave it forever. So we become scouts.

There's a lot of satisfaction in scouting. You watch a kid grow. You watch him from the time he's sixteen or seventeen and playing for some high school team, right up to his first years, if he's made it, in the majors.

Sometimes, though, the job is hard, especially when I have to tell some ambitious parent that his son is a good ball-player but he just doesn't have what it takes for the majors. You watch someone's dreams go out the window and that's always tough.

Baseball's always been important to me. As a kid, I was at every game I could get to. Then, I pitched for eleven years in the minors. I must have played ball for seven or eight different clubs during those years. And now I'm a scout.

People say football has become America's favorite sport. Maybe so—but baseball's mine.

33

POLICEMAN

POLICEMAN

John Flandon

There's something selfish about how most people earn a living. But being a policeman, you really know you're doing a job that needs to be done.

I became a policeman because it was a good opportunity for someone who didn't have a college education. I started out as a foot patrolman. I worked in a tough part of the city. And a lot of the time, I was scared. There was action every night.

I was stabbed once. Three guys were robbing a pharmacy. I saw two of them and I had them where I wanted them. But this third guy—he just came up from behind. Luckily, I had a 10-13 called on me. That's when someone from the community calls in for help.

After that, I worked in vice and gambling, a special unit. I worked in plain clothes, in undercover assignments. We broke up bookies, dice games, narcotics operations.

Now I'm in a patrol car. You ride around, answer calls, patrol the area, tell people their cars are illegally parked. It's ok for awhile. But now it's starting to be a little boring. When you're on a beat, when you're on foot, you know everyone in the neighborhood. You really get a relationship going with the people. But being in the cruiser, things are less personal. People feel you're more of an intruder in their community than someone who's part of it.

I've been thinking of getting into emergency service. Those are the rescue squads of the police force, the guys who go out on special calls. If someone is trapped under a train, or if some psycho has just killed ten people and is now holed up in some building, it's the emergency service patrolmen who get the call. Those are the guys with the bullet-proof vests and the sniper rifles, the guys who climb onto bridges to save jumpers.

As a policeman gets older, many of them want to get off the street and into an easier job back at the station. After awhile, maybe all the danger gets to you. You risk your life every day. It's usually the young guys who are gung ho. They want to make all the arrests. The older guys, a lot of them need to take it easier.

I'm not sure exactly what I want now. Maybe the emergency squad because that's always busy. In eight hours, you might go out a dozen times. But one thing I do know. I don't want an easy assignment. I don't want to work traffic. I don't even consider that a job.

Being a policeman gives me the challenge that I need. Some guys can just do any job, make a living, and go home every night. I can't understand that. I need to do a job that makes me feel good about myself, that makes me feel I'm doing something for people. Otherwise, why waste your time?

34

MAYOR

MAYOR

David Musante

I've been in politics for the last sixteen years. I spent six years on the city council and then the next nine years as a county commissioner. Now I'm starting my first term as a mayor.

This is my third week in office and I haven't had a day off yet. I'm working twelve hours a day, seven days a week. But I've never been happier in my life.

I started my political career by attending a P.T.A. meeting at one of the local grammar schools. Our schools were over-crowded back then. They were so crowded, in fact, that some of the classrooms were right near the boiler rooms. And that was something that angered everyone. Well, after that meeting, on the way home, I was talking to my wife. I told her how upset I was about the schools being so crowded. And she said, 'Don't just talk about it. Do something.' Then and there, I decided to run for the city council. I felt I wanted to be active in changing things. I didn't want to just sit back and let things happen.

Eventually, I brought in a resolution to study the building of an addition to one of our schools. But it was defeated by the city council and the mayor. I didn't stop there, though. I wrote an article in the local paper and spoke to the local P.T.A. groups. And finally, an addition to our town high school was built. Today, whenever I go by that school on the way home, I feel very good about it, very proud.

My advice to children is: If you want to do something, don't just talk about it. Get out there and do it.

The best thing about my job is that it's a chance to help people. I can really do things to make our town a better community to live in. But the worst thing is that you can kill yourself in the process because there are so many things to do. It's an exhausting job.

If you're young, you can get involved in politics mainly by working during campaigns. It's really helpful to a candidate if there are people who'll go out and help them distribute their literature. Kids can learn about the political issues by doing this. I myself have six kids and they all helped me during my campaign. They did telephone callings and literature drops.

It's exciting work being a mayor. The decisions you make have an effect on the lives of the people in your town. You really can get out there and change things.

35

THERAPIST

THERAPIST

Vivian Weiss

I used to be an actress. I loved acting but I found that when you act, you get very involved in thinking only about yourself. You think about two things all the time: about the character you're playing and about yourself. You really spend very little time thinking about other people. And I found that thinking about myself all the time was boring.

I knew I was curious about how other people lived. I wasn't only interested in myself or in the make-believe characters I played. I was also very interested in real people. And I felt that through therapy I could go beyond myself. I could reach out to a lot of other people.

Therapy is helping people to talk about their problems. It's helping them to talk about their problems and to then hopefully do something to make their problems better.

In a lot of ways, therapy is similar to acting. It's very dramatic. You're talking with people who are undergoing tremendous changes in their lives. They're often going through a real life crisis. And there are some people who have big, gigantic problems that have been secrets for many, many years. When they share these secrets with you, that can be very exciting and very dramatic.

I guess I like the contact that therapy gives me with people. I feel that I can really touch people's lives and they can touch mine. I've seen that a lot of the time when people talk to each other, they don't really talk about very special, important, private things. But being a therapist allows me to talk with people about these very real, very private areas. Businessmen and lawyers, for instance, don't usually speak so openly with their clients.

I work with little kids, with grown-ups, and with adolescents who are having a hard time with some of the changes in their lives. And a lot of the work I do is working with people who are sick or dying. These are people of all ages.

Working with people who are dying seems very important. When someone is very sick—they may have cancer or some other disease—life becomes very lonely for them. Most people, even their closest family members, don't want to be around them. But it seems important to be able to spend time with these people. They're very lonely, maybe the most lonely people in the world.

There are a lot of different types of therapists. You've already read about a dance therapist (see page 100). But psychologists, social workers, and psychiatrists are also considered therapists.

36

AUTHOR

AUTHOR

Steve Berman

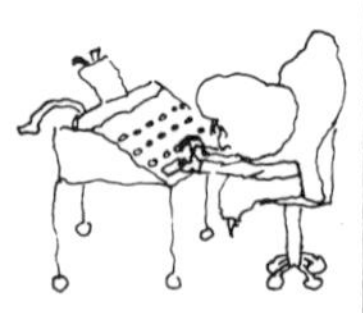

I had a dream one night and in the dream someone asked me, 'Why do you write?' My answer was: 'To share the different things I'm interested in.'

I did a lot of things before I actually became a writer. I owned a farm in Tennessee. I painted houses. I even worked as a butler for one of the wealthiest women in America.

Then, when I was twenty-five, I wrote a story about that experience, about being a butler. It was a funny story and I was able to sell it to a magazine. That's when my career as a professional writer began.

Writing was something I always knew I had a talent for. Even when I was a teenager, I loved writers. I idolized Ernest Hemingway who was a famous writer. I used to dress the way he dressed. My father even bought me a pipe because I told him Ernest Hemingway sometimes smoked a pipe.

In high school and in college, writing was my main interest. But, back then, I was more interested in the *idea* of being a writer than in actually becoming one. I wasn't brave enough yet to see if I really could be a writer.

When I started my career, I wrote articles for newspapers and magazines. I wrote stories about all sorts of things—about robots, modern-day pirates, athletes. Then, because I found out that it was hard to make a living just from writing these articles, I started to write books. I wrote a travel book, a book about all the free things you could visit in New England. Then, I wrote a book about nature, a guide to the outdoors. And after I met my wife, I wanted to write a book about love. So I spent two years travelling around America with my wife, speaking with hundreds of people about their marriages.

I'm the sort of person who's always becoming interested in new things. Being a writer allows me the time and the money to explore these new and always changing interests.

As I get older, though, the things I choose to write about are very different from the things I used to write about when I first started out. But what never changes is my fascination with words and with how I can combine these words to tell a better and better story.

I think I wrote this particular book because I wanted to know how other people became what they became; when I was growing up, I didn't know you could become so many different things.

EPILOGUE

With a tape recorder and a lot of curiosity, we visited dozens of people. We were interested in knowing *why* and *how* people become what they become. Why does one person, for instance, become a newspaper publisher while another chooses a career in farming, or in furniture making.

We came to certain conclusions:

We discovered that the work people did was very often related to their childhood hobbies. So it wasn't surprising to us that the comic book salesman we interviewed had been an avid comic book collector as a kid. Or that the movie theater owner used to watch all the old movies on television. Or that the clothing designer had made her own dolls' clothes as a girl.

Something else we learned was that no one liked their job all the time. Every job had its good and bad points. Being a chef, for example, is interesting work but it's also exhausting. Or being a freelance illustrator is very creative; unfortunately, it's not always profitable.

We also met a lot of people who had changed their jobs. Two social workers became the owners of a homemade ice cream parlor. An auto mechanic became a greenhouse foreman. A college teacher bought a movie house. "Switching careers," the vocational counselor we interviewed told us, "is becoming more and more popular."

We learned that everyone we interviewed worked hard at their profession. There's no getting around hard work. The violin maker we interviewed worked seven days a week, twelve to fourteen hours a day. The macrobiotic chef spent more time in his restaurant's kitchen than anywhere else.

Only with hard work, we saw, can there be deep satisfaction.

We hope our book has been helpful to you. And we hope this book has made you see that—
—If there's something you love doing, then do it. If you love doing something enough and if you do it well enough, you'll be able to turn it into a career. Even reading comics or eating ice cream can become careers.

Steve Berman
Vivian Weiss

INDEX